Test Yo

or.

The Highway Code

Includes 1993 Highway Code revisions

---

by

Geoffrey Whitehead, B.Sc. (Econ.)

Second Edition

Revised

Shaw & Sons

Published and printed in Great Britain by
Shaw & Sons Limited
Shaway House
21 Bourne Park
Bourne Road
Crayford
Kent DA1 4BZ

© Shaw & Sons Limited 1993

First published 1977
Revised 1979
Revised 1987
Revised 1989
Revised 1991
Second Edition .... July 1992
Revised .... October 1993

ISBN 0 7219 0695 8

© Crown copyright material is reproduced with the
permission of the Controller of HMSO

*No part of this publication may be reproduced
or transmitted in any form without the written
permission of the copyright holder*

This book is not a substitute for the Highway Code, which is an authoritative official publication. Instead, this book presents the rules contained in the Highway Code in a novel question and answer form, which can be studied by self-tuition methods, or can be handed to someone else – the wife – or your husband – or the boyfriend, with the request "Will you test me?" Practice makes perfect.

After a number of successful reprints, the book has been completely re-set in a more modern and 'user-friendly' style and the opportunity has been taken to introduce the most recent developments which embody the latest thinking about road safety in the 1993 Highway Code. While every effort has been made to ensure the accuracy of the present text, neither the author nor the publishers can accept responsibility for liabilities incurred due to any misunderstanding or misinterpretation of this book.

The author and publishers acknowledge gratefully the permission given by the Controller of Her Majesty's Stationery Office to reproduce the signs used in the Code.

These days many people are sensitive about 'sexist' words and phrases. For example the word 'driver' may refer to both men and women, but it would be tedious to use he/she and him/her throughout the text. The law recognises no distinction between the sexes (Interpretation Act 1978); where a male word is used it also means the female word, and vice versa. Accordingly the masculine pronoun has been used throughout this text, with apologies to those who are sensitive on this point.

The 1993 Highway Code frequently uses the words '**must**' and '**must not**' in bold type. These words show that the matter referred to is a legal requirement. Failure to observe the rule is an offence.

The important thing for the learner driver is to understand not only the wording of, but also the spirit behind, the Code. The Code is based upon courtesy to other road users, consideration for the safety of the general public and your passengers, and a determination on the part of all right-minded citizens to ensure pleasurable, safe motoring with the minimum interference with the natural environment, which is our mutual heritage.

THE GENERAL PATTERN OF ROAD SIGNS

Questions

1. What are the general patterns of road signs and what do they mean?

2. What are the two types of circles and what do they mean?

(a)   (b)   (c)

3. What do these signs mean?

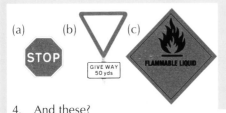

(a)   (b)   (c)

STOP   GIVE WAY 50 yds   FLAMMABLE LIQUID

4. And these?

5. What are the general patterns of direction signs?

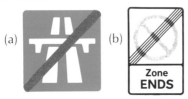

(a)   (b)   Zone ENDS

6. What does a line mean through any sign?

7. Mark up the check list at the front of the book.

Answers

1. (a) Circles give orders.
    (b) Triangles give warnings.
    (c) Rectangles give information.
    (d) Diamonds mean danger.

2. (a) A red circle prohibits; telling me what I may not do.
    (b) A blue circle gives a positive instruction; telling me what I must do.

3. (a) A red prohibitory circle. No goods vehicles over the maximum gross weight shown (in tonnes).
    (b) A blue (positive instruction) sign. It is compulsory to give way to vehicles from the right at this mini-roundabout.
    (c) A warning triangle – loose chippings after road resurfacing. A warning to reduce speed.

4. (a) This is the red octagon. It means 'Stop and Give Way to traffic on the major road ahead'.
    (b) This is the inverted triangle sign. It warns of a need to 'Give Way' ahead.
    (c) One of the 'diamonds for danger' signs. If a spillage occurs I should keep well away and summon the police and fire brigade.

5. (a) Rectangles give direction information about the road ahead.
    (b) At junctions, one end of a directional sign points the direction out with an arrow shape.
    (c) Blue backgrounds for general information.
    (d) Green backgrounds for primary routes.
    (e) White backgrounds with black borders for non-primary routes.
    (f) White backgrounds with blue borders for routes of local interest only.
    (g) Brown backgrounds with white lettering for tourist attractions.
    (h) White backgrounds with red borders for Ministry of Defence installations.

6. It means that a previously existing situation has ended. In these cases they are (a) motorway driving and (b) the controlled parking zone.

Questions	Answers

1. What does this sign mean?

1. Stop and give way, so
   (a) I stop at the solid white line.
   (b) I select first gear, set the gas, find the biting point and take effective observation, preparatory to moving off.

2. What does a blue circle with no red border mean on a road sign?

2. They are mostly signs which give positive instructions, rather than instructions of a prohibitory nature.

 (b) (c)

3. What do these blue signs mean?

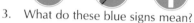

3. (a) A blue 30 sign shows a 'minimum speed of 30 m.p.h.', unlike the usual red circle 30 sign, which shows the maximum speed.
   (b) This sign shows the end of the minimum speed of 30 m.p.h., so that I may now slow down below 30 m.p.h.
   (c) Ahead only.

(a) (b) (c)

4. What do these blue circles mean?

4. (a) Keep left (or right if the symbol is reversed).
   (b) Pass either side.
   (c) Route to be used by pedal cycles only.

(a) (b)

5. What do these blue circle signs mean (and what would they mean if the symbols were reversed)?

5. (a) Turn left (turn right if reversed).
   (b) Turn left ahead (turn right ahead if symbol was reversed).

(a) (b) (c)

6. What do these signs mean?

6. (a) Weight limited to 20 tonnes.
   (b) No motor vehicles except solo motorcycles and mopeds.
   (c) Axle weight limited to 2 tonnes.

(a) (b) (c)

7. What do these compulsory signs mean?

7. (a) No right turn.
   (b) No left turn.
   (c) No U turn.

8. Tick up the check list.

Questions	Answers
1. What is the significance of a red triangle on a road sign?	1. A triangle warns of a possible hazard ahead.
2. What action do you take when you see a red triangle?	2. No action necessarily, but I must be alert and drive defensively, and adjust my speed, position etc., according to road and traffic conditions.

3. What should you do when you see a bend to the right (or left) sign?

3. Slow down if necessary and change down a gear.

4. What do these signs mean?

4. (a) Traffic signals ahead.
(b) Humped back bridge ahead.
(c) Uneven road surface ahead.

5. What do these signs mean?

5. (a) Crossroads ahead.
(b) Roundabout ahead.
(c) T junction ahead, with the main route bearing left.

6. And these?

6. (a) Slippery road ahead.
(b) Staggered junction ahead.
(c) Road narrows on both sides.

7. And these?

7. (a) Two-way traffic crosses a one-way road.
(b) and (c) Traffic merges from left (or right) with equal priority.

8. How many did you get right? Tick up the check list.

Questions	Answers

 (a) (b) (c)

1. What do these signs mean?

1. (a) Pedestrians crossing ahead.
(b) Cyclists and mopeds prohibited.
(c) Overtaking prohibited.

 (a) (b) (c)

2. What do these signs mean?

2. (a) Vehicles over the height shown are prohibited.
(b) Opening or swing bridge.
(c) Quayside or riverbank.

 (a) (b) (c)

3. What do these signs mean?

3. (a) Road narrows on offside (nearside if symbol is reversed). Plate may indicate single file traffic only.
(b) Side road entering from right (left if side reversed).
(c) No pedestrians.

 (a) (b) (c)

4. What do these signs mean?

4. (a) Overhead electric cable; a plate fixed to the post indicates the maximum safe height for vehicles.
(b) No motor vehicles.
(c) Manually operated temporary 'stop' sign.

 (a) (b) (c)

5. What do these signs mean?

5. (a) Dual carriageway ends.
(b) Steep hill downwards – gradient one in ten (10%).
(c) Steep hill upwards – gradient one in five (20%).

 (a) (b)

6. What do these signs mean?

6. (a) Humps in the road ahead.
(b) Advance warning of a series of humps.

7. Mark up the check list.

SIGNALS

Questions	Answers
1. When should you give signals?	1. When they will help or warn other drivers.
2. In what two ways can you signal?	2. (a) Arm signals. (b) Direction indicator signals.
3. What does this sign mean?	3. (a) I intend to move out to the right, or (b) I intend to turn right,
4. What does the flashing right hand amber indicator mean?	4. (a) I intend to move out to the right, or (b) I intend to turn right.
5. What does a circling right hand signal indicate?	5. (a) I intend to turn left. (b) I intend to move in to the left.
6. What does a flashing left hand amber indicator mean?	6. (a) I intend to turn left. (b) I intend to move in to the left. (c) I intend to stop on the left.
7. When should a driver use this signal, lowering and raising his right arm?	7. When he is going to slow down, or stop – for example at a pedestrian crossing.
8. What lighting indication warns drivers behind that a car ahead is going to slow down or stop?	8. The red brake warning lights go on automatically when the brake pedal is depressed.
9. Practice the hand signals in front of a mirror. Remember to check your indicator lights and brake lights at the start of every journey. Tick the check list at the front of the book when you complete this page.	

Questions	Answers
1. What are the three rules for giving hand signals?	
	1. (a) I must make sure I give the correct signal. (b) Give it clearly. (c) Give it in good time.
2. What are the three rules for giving indicator signals?	
	2. (a) Give the correct signal. (b) Give it in good time. (c) Make sure I cancel it after the manoeuvre is completed.
3. What should you do about the signals of other drivers and riders?	
	3. Act on them promptly, but remember I am still responsible for my own actions.
4. Who would need to know that you want to turn right?	
	4. A policeman, traffic warden or other person controlling traffic, all other road users and pedestrians.
5. What does this signal tell a policeman controlling traffic?	
	5. I wish to go straight ahead.
6. What does this signal tell a policeman controlling traffic?	
	6. I wish to turn left.
7. What are the Highway Code's three rules for moving off?	
	7. (a) Always look round as well as using the mirror. (b) Signal before moving out. (c) Move off when it is safe to do so, making sure not to cause other road users to change speed and direction.
8. Who is the police officer ordering to stop? 	
	8. A vehicle approaching from the front of the officer.
9. Repeat these until you know them. Practice the hand signals clearly in front of a mirror. Tick the check list at the front of the book.	

Questions	Answers

1. Who is being ordered to stop by this police officer?

1. Both vehicles directly ahead and vehicles behind the officer.

2. What is this policeman doing?

2. Calling traffic on from behind him.

3. And this one?

3. Calling traffic on that is in front of him.

4. And this one?

4. Calling traffic on from the side.

5. Mark up the check list at the front of the book.

POLICE POWERS

Questions

1. Who is being ordered to stop by this officer?

2. Who has authority to control traffic?

3. When should you give way to police cars, ambulances and fire engines?

4. A police officer signals you to stop. Must you obey him?

5. It is night time but you forget to switch on your lights. Have you committed an offence?

6. What are the rules about reckless driving?

7. Your engine is burning oil. What is the law on this?

8. What is the rule about overloading a passenger vehicle?

9. You have been ill and receiving treatment. Although you feel very poorly you decide to drive. Have you committed an offence?

10. You exhaust is leaking and the fumes are affecting the interior of the car. What is the rule?

11. Mark up the check list.

Answers

1. The traffic behind the officer.

2. (a) A uniformed police officer.
   (b) A traffic warden.
   (c) A school crossing patrol.

3. When their blue lights are flashing and their bells, or two-tone horns or sirens are sounding.

4. Yes – it is an offence to fail to stop when required to do so by a police officer, a traffic warden or a school crossing patrol.

5. Yes – under the Road Transport Lighting Act.

6. It is an offence to drive recklessly or at a speed or in a manner which is dangerous to the public.

7. It is an offence to drive a vehicle which emits excessive fumes and smoke.

8. It is an offence to carry passengers in such numbers or in such a manner as to cause danger.

9. The Code says I should not drive if I am not well. It is an offence to drive under the influence of drugs or medicine. I should take a taxi.

10. It is an offence to drive with an inefficient exhaust system.

THE ROAD USER AND ANIMALS

Questions	Answers

1. What are the rules for driving past animals?

    1. (a) Give them plenty of room.
        (b) Drive slowly.
        (c) Be ready to stop if necessary.
        (d) Do not blow the horn, or rev the engine.

2. When are animals likely to be encountered without warning?

    2. After a left-hand bend or brow of a hill.

3. What are the dangers when animals are in a car?

    3. (a) They may disturb or distract me while I am driving.
        (b) They may escape on to the highway if I stop for any reason.

(a)  (b) (c)

4. What do these signs mean?

    4. (a) Cattle crossing ahead.
        (b) Wild animals possibly straying on the road ahead.
        (c) Sheep straying.

5. And this sign?

    5. Accompanied horses crossing ahead.

6. You are approaching a hump-backed bridge. A farmer's boy flags you down. What is the likely reason?

    6. The Highway Code says that anyone driving cattle or other animals should if possible send someone ahead to bends in the road, or hump-back bridges, to warn drivers. The road ahead is probably full of cattle.

7. The law recognises certain animals as valuable property, and requires you to stop if you cause injury to them. What animals are these?

    7. Horses, cattle, asses, mules, sheep, pigs, goats and dogs.

8. What must you do beside stopping?

    8. (a) Give my own name and address to anyone requiring it.
        (b) Give the vehicle owner's name and address, and the registration number.
        (c) If no-one is about, report the accident to the police within 24 hours.
        (d) Produce my certificate of insurance to anyone who requires it, or to the police when I report it, or if I do not have it with me produce it within 5 days to a police station.

9. You have a dog in your car, and you breakdown on a motorway. What is the rule?

    9. Animals should be kept in the vehicle wherever possible. If not, I must use a lead.

10. Mark up the check list.

THE MOTORCYCLIST AND MOPED RIDER

Questions	Answers
1. What particular items of equipment are of especial importance to motorcyclists and riders?	
	1. The safety helmet, sturdy boots, gloves and fluorescent or reflective materials.
2. When must you wear a helmet?	
	2. On all journeys, fastened securely, and of approved design.
3. Who else must wear a safety helmet?	
	3. My pillion passenger.
4. How many passengers are allowed on a two-wheel machine?	
	4. Only one.
5. How must a passenger sit?	
	5. Astride the vehicle, on a proper seat securely fitted behind the driver's seat, and with proper rests for the feet.
6. What part of your machine must conform particularly with regulations?	
	6. The exhaust system and silencer must be of an approved type.
7. Where must you park a motorcycle/moped in a meter zone?	
	7. In the specially marked motorcycle part, or (when permitted) at a meter.
8. Which roads are forbidden to low powered motorcycles?	
	8. Motorways.
9. Why is a sound knowledge of the Code and strict observance of it very important to motorcyclists?	
	9. Because we are more vulnerable than other drivers.
10. Where must riders be particularly careful of pedestrians?	
	10. In queues of traffic where we are overtaking and pedestrians may be crossing between vehicles.
11. How many did you get right? Mark up the check list at the front of the book.	

Questions	Answers

1. What precautions should a driver take when pedestrians are about?

    1. (a) Drive carefully and slowly.
    (b) Be wary of pedestrians when passing buses or stationary mobile shops.
    (c) Be wary of parked vehicles at all times. Pedestrians may emerge.

2. Which groups need particular care?

    2. (a) The blind, and the deaf-blind.
    (b) The old, who may take longer to cross the road.

(a) (b)

    (c) Disabled or infirm persons.
    (d) Young people.

3. What do these signs mean?

    3. (a) School crossing patrol.

4. Describe the warning sign erected near a school?

    (b) Pedestrians in the road ahead.

    4. (a) It is a red triangle sign.
    (b) It shows children running.
    (c) It may have a plate showing 'school'.
    (d) It may have a plate warning of a crossing patrol.

    (e) At places of particular danger there may be a flashing amber light to warn of a crossing patrol ahead.

5. What does this marking on the surface of the road mean?

    5. Keep entrance clear of stationary vehicles, even if picking up and setting down children.

6. When has a pedestrian the right of way on the road?

    6. When he is on a crossing.

7. A pedestrian is waiting at a zebra crossing. Must the motorist give way?

    7. No, but if the pedestrian does move onto the zebra crossing he will at once have the right of way.

8. What is the safest rule for approaching a zebra crossing?

    8. Approach pedestrian crossings with extreme caution. Be prepared to give way. Signal to drivers when intending to slow down, or stop.

9. What extra care is required on wet or icy roads?

    9. It may take longer to slow down or stop. Give myself extra time by reducing speed early and keep a greater distance from the vehicle in front.

10. Tick the check list.

MORE ABOUT PEDESTRIAN CROSSINGS

Questions

1. What are the two types of pedestrian crossings?

2. A crossing is controlled by lights, or by police or traffic wardens. What do you do about pedestrians still on the crossing when the signal is given for vehicles to move?

3. What does this flashing amber light mean and where would you see it?

4. What is special about a straight pelican crossing?

5. The Code says "Do not harass pedestrians at crossings". How might you harass them?

6. There is a queue of traffic beyond a pedestrian crossing. What must you do?

7. What does the Highway Code say about overtaking near a zebra crossing?

8. What does the Code say about signalling to pedestrians at a crossing?

9. One driver's signal is particularly important at pedestrian crossings. What is it?

10. Mark up the check list at the front of the book.

Answers

1. Zebra crossings and pelican crossings.

2. Give way to pedestrians who are still on the crossing.

3. At pelican crossings controlled by lights, the red light will be followed by this flashing amber light. I must give way to pedestrians still on the crossing, then I may proceed.

4. Even when there is a central refuge it is all one crossing. I must wait for people crossing from the other side of the refuge.

5. By revving my engine, making them afraid I was about to move off.

6. I must leave the crossing clear when I get to it, waiting until there is enough clear room for my vehicle on the far side of the crossing.

7. Never overtake when approaching a zebra crossing.

8. Do not signal to them to cross, another vehicle may be approaching.

9. The slowing down signal. It avoids 'shunting' accidents from the rear, and reassures pedestrians that you have noticed them waiting to cross.

15

MORE POINTS ABOUT PEDESTRIANS

Questions	Answers
1. There is no pavement. Where should pedestrians walk?	1. On the right hand side of the road facing oncoming traffic.
2. Which points are therefore particularly dangerous to pedestrians?	2. Left hand bends, where I may suddenly come upon them.
3. Processions, marching troops, etc. march on which side of the road?	3. The left side, as if they were a moving vehicle.
4. What precautions should the motorist take when such bodies of marching pedestrians are about?	4. (a) Give them as much room as possible. (b) Keep your speed down. (c) Take special care on left hand bends, where you may suddenly find them ahead of you.
5. You approach a junction at which you are turning left or right. There are pedestrians crossing the road you intend to turn into. What is the rule here?	5. Give way to pedestrians who are crossing at a junction where you are turning left or right.
6. When should you also give way to pedestrians?	6. When entering or emerging from property bordering the road.
7. What is an uncontrolled zebra crossing?	7. A crossing marked by black and white stripes, zigzag markings, and lighted beacons and at which there is no police officer controlling the traffic.
8. What is the rule about uncontrolled crossings?	8. Give precedence to pedestrians.
9. What do the zigzags before a pedestrian crossing indicate?	9. An area where it is forbidden: (a) to overtake a moving vehicle or (b) to overtake the leading vehicle which has stopped to give way to a pedestrian on the crossing, or (c) to park, or wait (except to give way to a pedestrian).
10. Who has precedence at push button controlled crossings?	10. A pedestrian on the crossing, even when the amber lights are flashing.
11. Mark up the check list.	

RULES OF THE ROAD

Questions	Answers
1. What is the rule of the road?	1. Keep to the left.
2. When do you move over to the right hand lane?	2. (a) When I intend to overtake. (b) When passing a stationary vehicle, or pedestrians walking along the road. (c) When I intend to turn right. (d) When road signs or markings tell me I should do so.
3. What do you do when vehicles are overtaking you?	3. (a) Allow them to do so freely. (b) Ease off the accelerator to give them more chance to pass me. (c) Allow them into the gap in front if they are in danger.
4. A single carriageway road has four lanes. What is the rule?	4. I must not use the lanes on the right hand half of the road unless signs and markings indicate that I may do so.
5. What is the routine drill used for all manoeuvres on the road?	5. Mirror-Signal-Manoeuvre. (M.S.M.)
6. What rule should you observe if a manoeuvre appears likely to be dangerous?	6. When in doubt, do not manoeuvre.
7. You feel very tired, but want to get to a destination because tomorrow you have an important appointment. What do you do?	7. The Code says "Do not start a journey if you are tired".
8. What must you do about speed limits?	8. Observe them, including those for my own class of vehicle.
9. What must you do about signals?	9. I must observe all signals, including those of police officers and traffic wardens controlling traffic.
10. You have been teaching a friend to drive and have L plates on your vehicle. What is the rule?	10. The code says L pates should be removed, or covered, when no-one is under instruction in the vehicle.
11. Mark up the check list.	

LINES ON THE ROAD

Questions	Answers
1. What colour are lines marked on the road?	1. White or yellow (or red for the new 'red routes').
2. What is the general significance of yellow lines?	2. They refer to parking regulations or box junctions (restricting entry to the junction).
3. What are the purposes of white lines on the road?	3. To guide, warn or give orders.
4. What warning lines appear on many roads?	4. Long white lines, with short gaps between.
5. What do they warn about?	5. They warn of hazards ahead.
6. May you cross a hazard warning line at any time?	6. Only when I can see the road well ahead to be clear.
7. What does a double white line in the centre of the road mean?	7. Do not cross or straddle the lines except in very special circumstances.
8. What are these special circumstances?	8. (a) When entering or leaving premises. (b) To enter or leave a side road. (c) When ordered to do so by a policeman or a traffic warden. (d) When avoiding an obstruction such as a broken-down vehicle or an accident.
9. What special precautions should be taken?	9. Take exceptional care that the road ahead is clear.
10. What road marking gives warning of double white lines ahead?	10. A white arrow head indicating that I should keep in to the left.
11. How many did you get right? Mark up the check list at the start of the book.	

Questions	Answers
1. Sometimes one of the double lines in the centre of the road is unbroken, but the other is broken. What does this mean?	
	1. Traffic on the side where the dashes are painted may cross the centre line to overtake if the way ahead is clear.
2. When crossing the centre line to overtake you must be sure about one point concerned with the overtaking manoeuvre. What is it?	
	2. That I can complete the manoeuvre before reaching an unbroken line on my own side.
3. What will help me to overtake quickly?	
	3. Dropping down a gear gives extra power.
4. What does the broken line not mean?	
	4. It does not mean it is safe to overtake. That will depend upon road and traffic conditions.
5. Sometimes areas of road are painted with diagonal strips, or chevrons. Why is this done?	
	5. (a) To separate lines of oncoming traffic at dangerous points. (b) To protect traffic up ahead in a turn-right lane.
6. What are the rules about this type of area with diagonal white lines?	
	6. Do not drive on these areas if I can avoid doing so.
7. Suppose the chevron has a solid white edge line to it?	
	7. In that case I may only enter the area in an emergency.
8. What are centre lines like on minor roads?	
	8. Evenly spaced medium length dashes.
9. What is the purpose of such lines?	
	9. (a) They guide motorists when approaching bends, etc. (b) They are particularly useful in foggy or misty weather.
10. What are lane markings like?	
	10. They consist of very short white lines.
11. Which lane should you normally travel in?	
	11. In the left hand lane, unless I am going to overtake or turn right, or pass a parked vehicle.
12. Go over the page again. Tick up the check list at the start of the book.	

LANE DISCIPLINE

Questions	Answers

Questions

1. What are the rules for changing lanes?

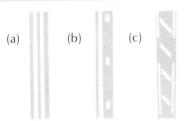

2. Identify these lines on the roads, and their meanings.

3. When is the centre lane to be used on a three lane single carriageway road?

4. Who has more right to use the centre lane, you or the oncoming traffic?

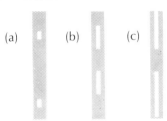

5. Identify these road markings.

6. Mark up the check list.

Answers

1. (a) Do not change unnecessarily from lane to lane.
(b) If I do need to change lanes I first use my mirror.
(c) If it is safe to move over I signal my intention well beforehand.
(d) I make sure I do not cause other drivers to swerve or slow down.

2. (a) Double white lines – no crossing except in very special circumstances.
(b) Double centre line, one broken, one unbroken – no crossing the centre line if the unbroken line is nearer the driver than the broken line.
(c) Hazard lines with diagonal stripes – do not enter the shaded area if I can avoid doing so.

3. When overtaking, or turning right.

4. Neither party has more right to use it than the other.

5. (a) Lane lines.
(b) Centre lines.
(c) Hazard warning lines.

Questions	Answers
1. What is the first rule for overtaking?	1. Never overtake unless it is safe for myself and other road users. Look out for cyclists and motorcyclists especially.
2. What about the road ahead?	2. Make sure that it is clear far enough ahead to complete the overtaking manoeuvre.
3. And the road behind?	3. That should also be clear of overtaking vehicles. Especial care is needed on fast roads. I must use my mirror.
4. What should a motorcyclist also do?	4. Turn his head to look behind.
5. When is it most difficult to judge the speed of approaching vehicles?	5. At dusk and in darkness, mist or fog.
6. What is the correct sequence for the actual overtaking manoeuvre?	6. Mirror - Signal - Manoeuvre.
7. Once you have started to overtake what should you do?	7. (a) Move quickly past the slower vehicle. (b) Leaving it plenty of room, move back into lane in front of it.
8. When is it permissible to overtake on the left of another vehicle?	8. (a) When the driver in front has indicated he means to turn right. (b) When I want to turn left at a junction. (c) When traffic is moving slowly in queues, and the vehicles in the right hand lane are moving more slowly than in my lane. (d) In one way streets.
9. What size gap should be left between you and the vehicle in front of you?	9. A gap of 1 metre for each mph of speed, or a two-second time gap, is about right.
10. Mark up the check list.	

Questions	Answers
1. On a three lane dual carriageway what are the uses of the three lanes? First the inside lane?	1. It is the normal lane for traffic.
2. And the middle lane?	2. This lane is for overtaking slower vehicles. I may stay in it if I am overtaking a succession of slower vehicles but I must return to the inside lane when the road is clear.
3. And the third lane?	3. The third lane is for overtaking only or for traffic turning right. I must return to the middle lane after using it, without cutting in.
4. What do these signs mean?	4. One way traffic only in the direction shown.
5. What are the rules for using one way streets? First about the lanes?	5. Choose the correct lane for my exit as soon as possible.
6. What indication may be given to indicate the lanes?	6. The road may be marked – for example with the words 'King's Cross' on a particular lane.
7. If there are no special markings what lanes do you use?	7. (a) Left hand lane for a left hand exit. (b) Right hand lane for a right hand exit. (c) Any lane for a straight ahead exit.
8. What is the difficulty in very narrow single track roads?	8. Passing is only possible at special passing places.
9. When should you pull into a passing place?	9. (a) When a vehicle is approaching. (b) When another vehicle wishes to overtake.
10. Suppose the passing place is not on your side!	10. I wait opposite it.
11. Who requires special consideration?	11. A vehicle travelling up-hill.
12. What is the rule about buses?	12. In towns I should give way to buses indicating an intention to move off - if I safely can do so.
13. Mark up the check list.	

Questions	Answers
1. How should you approach a junction?	
2. Before crossing or turning, what should you do?	1. With great care, and be ready to stop if necessary.
3. What is the chief danger when crossing a more important road?	2. Look right – look left – then right again.
4. Another driver signals that all is clear. What do you do?	3. It is important not to block the road, for example by stalling the car, or if my exit on the other side is not clear.
5. Whose signals may you rely upon?	4. Acknowledge his courtesy but do not rely on his signals. It is still my responsibility to ensure that it is safe to emerge.
6. What do double broken white lines mean at a junction?	5. Those of a police officer or traffic warden.
7. What other indication may there be at such junctions?	6. Prepare to give way by slowing down and be ready to stop if necessary. The major road has priority.
	7. There may be a 'Give Way' sign.
8. Here is the 'Give Way' sign. What does it mean?	
9. Describe the 'Stop' sign.	8. Give way; traffic crossing ahead of me has priority.
10. What must you do at the stop sign?	9. The sign is a red octagon with the word 'STOP' in white capitals. See page 5 for an illustration.
11. When is it safe to proceed?	10. I must stop at the solid white line.
12. How do we pass an island in the road?	11. When there is a large enough gap in the traffic for me to carry out the manoeuvre I am about to perform.
13. Tick up the check list.	12. On the left, unless road signs indicate otherwise.

MORE ABOUT JUNCTIONS

Questions	Answers
1. Where may you find directions about junctions ahead?	1. (a) On road signs at the side of the road. (b) On the lanes, as lane markings.
2. What are the vital points to consider when approaching a junction?	2. (a) Road position. (b) Speed. (c) The safety of vulnerable people; pedestrians, cyclists and motorcyclists.
3. What is the significance of these markings?	3. They tell me in advance how to position myself for exit from the next junction, when it is safe to proceed.
4. When is this sign most useful?	4. In foggy weather and at night since it pinpoints the 'Give Way' road position ahead.
5. What is the danger when long vehicles are turning right, or left, ahead of you?	5. They may need the whole width of the road to make their turn. I must give them plenty of room.
6. A vehicle approaching on your right on the major road you wish to enter is signalling that it intends to turn left? Is it safe to proceed?	6. No, I should wait to make sure.
7. What is this marking called?	7. It is a box junction.
8. What are the rules for entering box junctions?	8. (a) I must not enter the box junction unless my exit road or lane from it is clear. (b) But I may enter it if I am turning right and am only prevented from doing so by oncoming traffic.
9. Tick the check list.	

Questions	Answers
1. When turning right what is the sequence of actions you should take?	1. Mirror - Signal - Manoeuvre.
2. When and why should you use your mirror when turning right?	2. Well before I mean to turn right, so that I know the position and movement of traffic behind me.
3. Your mirror shows it is safe to begin your turn. What do you do first?	3. Signal my intention to turn right and assume the correct position on the road.
4. What is the correct position on the road?	4. (a) If there is a turn right lane I go to that lane. (b) In a wide road I take up position just left of the middle of the road, leaving room for traffic to pass on the left. (c) In a narrow road just left of the centre line, but I will be unable to avoid holding up traffic behind me.
5. How do you actually make your right turn, if an oncoming vehicle is also turning right?	5. (a) Normally we pass offside to offside. (b) If nearside passing is necessary I watch out for oncoming traffic hidden by the other vehicle.
6. On a dual carriageway where should you wait before turning right?	6. In the central reserve, out of the way of traffic on both halves of the road.
7. What is the rule about pedestrians when turning right (or left)?	7. I must give way to pedestrians crossing the road into which I am turning.
8. How should one cross a dual carriageway?	8. One should regard it as two separate roads. Wait in the central reserve until it is safe to enter the second half of the road.
9. Suppose the central reserve is too small for your vehicle?	9. I wait in the side road until I can cross in one movement.
10. Mark up the check list at the front of the book.	

SPEED LIMITS AND OTHER SIGNS

Questions	Answers
1. What is the rule about speed limits?	1. Never break the speed limits for the road you are on, or the vehicle you are driving.
2. You suspect you have missed a 30 m.p.h. sign. How can you tell whether there is a 30 m.p.h. limit?	2. If there are street lights I am probably in a 30 m.p.h. zone. I must slow down to that speed.
3. What speed limit should a good driver always set for himself?	3. He should never drive so fast that he cannot stop well within the distance that he can see to be clear.
4. The Code says "Bear in mind any speed limit is a maximum." What does this mean?	4. It means that because I see a sign saying '50' does not mean it is safe to drive at that speed. Safe speeds depend on road and traffic conditions.
5. What are 'national speed limits'?	5. A pattern of speed limits for certain vehicles. For cars 30 m.p.h in built up areas; 60 m.p.h. on single carriageways; 70 m.p.h. elsewhere.

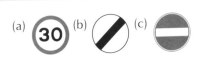

(a) (b) (c)

6. What do these signs mean?	6. (a) Maximum speed 30 m.p.h. (b) National speed limit applies. (c) No entry for motor vehicles.

(a) (b) (c)

7. What do these signs mean?	7. (a) How far it is to the hazard shown on the sign. (b) Falling or fallen rocks. (c) Low flying aircraft, or sudden aircraft noise.

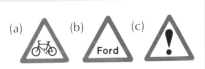

(a) (b) (c)

8. And these?	8. (a) Cycle route ahead. (b) This is a worded warning sign for a ford or water splash. Other worded signs are also used. (c) Hazard ahead. Look out for an unusual hazard. A plate will tell me what it is. For example a dust cloud.
9. How many did you get right? Put a tick on the check list at the front of this book.	

MORE ABOUT OVERTAKING

Questions	Answers

Questions

1. What should you do when someone is overtaking you?

2. A vehicle is stationary ahead of you on your side of a two-lane road. What should you do before passing it?

3. There are eleven places where you may not overtake. Where are they?

4. If in doubt ... (continue)

5. What is the rule about overtaking when traffic is queued up in lanes on a dual carriageway?

6. You are driving a slow moving vehicle on a narrow, winding road. Several vehicles are following behind. What is the rule?

7. Tick up the check list.

Answers

1. (a) I must not accelerate.
   (b) If necessary, ease off the accelerator, and slow down a little to let the overtaking vehicle pass more easily.

2. Give way to vehicles coming towards me.

3. (i) In the zig-zag area of a pedestrian crossing.
   (ii) At a road junction.
   (iii) At a corner, or bend in the road.
   (iv) At a hump-back bridge.
   (v) At the brow of a hill.
   (vi) At a level crossing.
   (vii) Where the road narrows.
   (viii) When to do so would force another vehicle to swerve or slow down.
   (ix) Where it would mean crossing unbroken double white lines, or double white lines with an unbroken line nearest to me.
   (x) Where a sign 'No overtaking' appears, and the restriction has not been lifted.
   (xi) Where it would mean driving over an area marked with diagonal stripes or chevrons.

4. ... do not overtake.

5. It is forbidden to move to a lane on my left to overtake. I may only do so if I wish to turn left or to park.

6. As soon as I can I should pull in, and slow down or stop, to allow them to overtake.

Questions	Answers
1. You are about to turn left. What do you do?	1. (a) Use the mirrors to assess the following traffic situation. (b) Well before the turn give a left turn signal. (c) Make the turn when it is safe to do so, without swinging out to the right before or after turning. (d) If crossing a cycle or bus lane look out for traffic using it.
2. What particular danger is there in a left turn?	2. A cyclist or motorcyclist may be coming up on my left hand side.
3. What is the rule when approaching a roundabout?	3. Give way to traffic from the right, unless road markings indicate otherwise.
4. What if the roundabout is clear?	4. Keep moving.
5. What does this diagram illustrate?	5. The recommended route round a roundabout for a vehicle turning left.
6. Explain the diagram.	6. The motorist intending to turn left approaches in the left hand lane, showing a left turn indicator. He uses the left hand lane on the roundabout and leaves by the left hand lane, showing left indicator all the time.
7. When might some modification to this recommended path be necessary?	7. (a) When the left hand approach lane is blocked. (b) When the left hand exit lane is blocked. (c) When road markings indicate otherwise.
8. Mark up the check list.	

MORE ABOUT ROUNDABOUTS

Questions	Answers

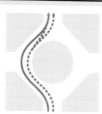

1.   Explain this diagram.

2.   What is the purpose of the dotted line?

3.   Explain the details of the dotted line.

4.   Explain this diagram.

5.   What is the dotted line indicating?

6.   Mark up the check list at the front of the book.

1.   It shows the recommended path round a roundabout for a vehicle going straight ahead.
(a) Approach in the left hand lane.
(b) Keep in the left hand lane while on the roundabout.
(c) Use the left hand indicator when passing the exit before the one you are taking.

2.   It shows the route to be taken if road conditions dictate (for example if the left hand lane is blocked).

3.   (a) Approach in the right hand lane.
(b) Keep in the right hand lane on the roundabout.
(c) Use the left turn indicator when passing the exist before the one you intend to take.
(d) Exit the roundabout in the left hand lane, if available.

4.   (a) It shows the path to be followed on a roundabout when turning right.
(b) Approach in the right hand lane.
(c) Indicate right turn as you approach the roundabout.
(d) Keep to the right lane in the roundabout, keeping right indicator on.
(e) Change to left turn indicator when passing the exit before the one to be taken.

5.   An alternative exit path if traffic conditions dictate.

ROUNDABOUTS AND REVERSING RULES

Questions	Answers
1. What special hazard is met on roundabouts?	
	1. Other motorists must cross in front of me as they head for their exits.
2. What precaution should you take?	2. Look out for vehicles signalling their intentions and show them courtesy where necessary.
3. Who needs to be shown especial courtesy?	
	3. (a) Cyclists (b) Motorcyclists (c) Long vehicles forced to take a special path both in the approach to and on the roundabout.
4. When there are more than two lanes at the entrance to a roundabout which one do you take?	
	4. The clearest and most convenient lane both on the approach and through the roundabout – bearing in mind the exit I intend to use.
5. There are now places where two, or even three, roundabouts occur together. How should you deal with them?	
	5. By applying the normal rules for roundabouts, and keeping a special look-out for the give way lines.
6. Who needs special consideration?	6. The vehicle crossing ahead of me to reach its exit lane.
7. What precautions should you take before reversing?	
	7. Ensure that no pedestrians, especially children, or obstructions are in the road behind me.
8. Which spots require especial care?	
	8. Those parts of the road to the side and rear of the car which cannot be seen in a rear view mirror. In any case, I should always turn round to look and not rely on my mirror when reversing.
9. If in doubt what do you do?	
	9. Get out of the car and look, or get someone to guide me.
10. Where must a vehicle not reverse?	
	10. From a side road into a main road.
11. Most cars are fitted with reversing lights. What is the advantage?	
	11. (a) In the dark I can see behind. (b) At all times other drivers are warned that I am reversing.
12. Tick up the check list.	

HORNS, CAR TELEPHONES AND LIGHTS

Questions	Answers
1. What is the purpose of sounding the horn?	1. To let another road user know I am there.
2. When may you not sound your horn?	2. (a) When my vehicle is stationary, unless there is danger from another (moving) vehicle. (b) Between 23.30 and 07.00 hrs. in a built up area.
3. Another driver breaks the rules and puts you in hazard. Should you hoot at him?	3. The Code says "Never use the horn as a rebuke".
4. What is the rule about car telephones?	4. (a) Do not use a hand-held microphone or telephone handset whilst the vehicle is moving. (b) Do not speak into a hands-free microphone if it distracts you from your driving.
5. What are the rules about the lights on the car?	5. All the lamps must be clean, in working order, and the headlights must be correctly adjusted. I must switch on at lighting-up time.
6. What do you do when dazzled?	6. Slow down, or stop.
7. At what speed should you drive in the dark?	7. So that I can stop well within the distance my headlights show to be clear.
8. What lights should you use at night in a built up area?	8. Dipped headlamps unless the street lighting is so good that they are not needed.
9. When should you dip your headlamps?	9. (a) When they might dazzle other drivers whether approaching me or ahead of me on my own side. (b) In fog I always drive with dipped headlights.
10. What does it mean when drivers flash their headlamps?	10. The Highway Code says that the only official meaning this can have is the same as sounding the horn – it lets me know they are there.
11. Tick up the check list at the front of the book.	

HEADLAMPS AND PARKING AT NIGHT

Questions	Answers
1. You are following another vehicle closely at night. What consideration should you have for the driver in front?	1. Even dipped headlamps will dazzle him in his mirrors if I am too close. I must fall back a little.
2. When should you use headlamps or front foglamps in daylight?	2. When visibility is seriously reduced (less than 100 metres) by fog, snow, smoke or heavy rain.
3. What does the Code say about lights on motorways at night?	3. Always use headlamps on fast roads, even if they are well lit.
4. When else should you use headlamps?	4. On roads where the street lamps are more than 185 metres (200 yards) apart, or are not lit.
5. What does the Code say about parking on the road at night?	5. Never park on the road at night if it can be avoided.
6. What vehicles may park unlit at nights?	6. Cars, light vans, invalid carriages and motorcycles.
7. Where may they park?	7. On roads which are subject to a 30 m.p.h. limit, but not within 10 metres of a junction or facing the wrong way, unless it is in a recognised parking place.
8. When is it particularly dangerous to park on the road?	8. In fog.
9. What must you do when parking in foggy conditions.	9. Leave the lights on at all times if I am forced to park on the road.
10. Who, in particular, must not park without lights on the road at night?	10. Drivers of vehicles with trailers or projecting loads.
11. Mark up the check list.	

PARKING AND WAITING

Questions	Answers
1. Where may you not park your vehicle, or let it stand?	
	1. There are many places, but they come under six headings. (a) Where a sign tells me not to wait, or I have been warned beforehand that I am entering a controlled parking zone. (b) Where it will obscure the view of other drivers. (c) Where it would be a danger to other road users. (d) Where it would inconvenience traffic or other road users. (e) Where emergency vehicles enter or leave premises, or stop. (f) Where it would make the road narrow.
2. List the signs that prohibit parking or waiting on the road.	
	2. (a) The 'no parking' sign. (b) Any clearway sign. (c) The bus lane sign. (d) Yellow lines on the edge of the road (but details are given on posts nearby or at the entry to a zone). (e) Double white lines in the centre of the road – even if one is broken.

3. What do these signs mean?	
	3. (a) Waiting restrictions apply. (b) Gives the times of 'no waiting' on the upper part, and the times when loading and unloading is not permitted (usually the rush hours). (c) Clearway – no stopping on the main carriageway.
4. What is this sign?	
	4. The urban clearway sign.
5. May you stop on an urban clearway?	
	5. Only for up to 2 minutes to set down or pick up passengers.
6. What does this sign mean?	
	6. I am entering a meter zone. Parking is only permitted at a meter after payment of the necessary charge.
7. You enter a meter zone after the time shown on the plate. What is your position?	
	7. Bay parking only, without charge.
8. Tick up the check list.	

ROAD MARKINGS ABOUT PARKING

Questions	Answers
1. What colour are the lines that refer to parking, or waiting restrictions?	
	1. Yellow.
2. Where are they situated?	
	2. Along the edge of the carriageway.
3. What is the general nature of these yellow line restrictions?	
	3. No waiting, except for loading and unloading or for passengers to board and alight, during times shown on nearby plates.
4. What does a single continuous yellow line mean?	
	4. Restrictions for at least 8 hours a day between 7 am and 7 pm and on four or more days a week.
5. What does a double yellow line mean?	
	5. The restrictions last even longer, as shown on the plates (eg 'At any time' means a continuous prohibition).
6. What does a broken yellow line mean?	
	6. It means that waiting is restricted at other times than the normal working day – for instance it may be restricted during rush hours.
7. What further restrictions do pavement bands impose?	
	7. Yellow bands on pavements restrict the right of vehicles to load and unload at times shown on plates nearby.

(a)   (b)   (c)

8. Explain these pavement stripes.

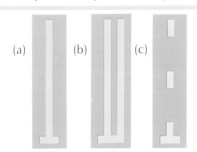

(a)   (b)   (c)

9. Identify these parking stripes.

10. Mark up the check list at the front of the book.

8. (a) Two pavement bands mean that loading is prohibited during the normal working day.
(b) Three pavement bands mean loading and unloading is prohibited during normal working time and other times as well. For example the plate may say 'No loading at any time'.
(c) One band means loading is prohibited for shorter periods – usually rush hours.

9. (a) 'No waiting' for at least 8 hours between 7 am and 7 pm.
(b) 'No waiting' for at least 8 hours and plate may say longer.
(c) 'No waiting' for shorter periods.

MORE ABOUT PARKING

Questions	Answers
1. Where would parking obscure the view of other drivers?	
	1. (a) At a junction. (b) At a bend. (c) At the brow of a hill. (d) At a hump back bridge.
2. Where would parking be a danger to other users of the road or to pedestrians?	
	2. (a) At or near a bus stop. (b) On the carriageway of a pedestrian crossing, marked by zig-zags. (c) At or near a school entrance. (d) On a footpath, pavement or cycle path. (e) On the right hand side of a road at night – except in a one-way street. (f) Where it would obscure a traffic sign. (g) On or near a level crossing.
3. Where would parking hold up traffic or inconvenience others?	
	3. (a) On a narrow road. (b) On flyovers, in tunnels or underpasses (unless notices permit). (c) On fast main roads (except in a lay-by). (d) On motorways (except in emergencies on the hard shoulder). (e) On a single track road, or in a passing place on such a narrow road. (f) Outside a private entrance for vehicles. (g) Blocking the entrance or exit to a car park. (h) Where it prevents the use of a properly parked vehicle. (i) On a bus lane or cycle lane. (j) Where the kerb has been lowered to help wheel-chair users.
4. Where might parking interfere with the emergency services?	
	4. (a) Outside hospital entrances. (b) Outside doctors' entrances. (c) Outside fire stations. (d) Near a fire hydrant in the road. (e) At the entrance to police stations. (f) At the entrance to coastguard stations.
5. Tick up the check list at the front of the book.	

MORE ABOUT PARKING

Questions	Answers
1. Where might parking make the road too narrow?	
	1. (a) Opposite a traffic island. (b) Alongside another parked vehicle (double parking). (c) Opposite a vehicle parked on the other side of the road – if this narrows the road to less than two vehicle widths. (d) Near road works.
2. What is the general rule for parking?	
	2. Make sure to park the vehicle safely. Walk a few yards rather than cause an accident.
3. When you park you will leave the vehicle. How should you do so?	
	3. By the side nearest the pavement whenever possible.
4. Who else should always alight on the pavement side?	
	4. The passengers, especially children.
5. What particular danger arises as you leave a vehicle?	
	5. When doors are opened suddenly they may cause an accident.
6. What is a disc zone?	
	6. A special zone where parking is permitted only to vehicles which display a parking disc. Times and days of operation are shown at entries to the zone.
7. Is it permitted to stop in a bus lane or cycle lane?	
	7. Only to load and unload goods.
8. Is it permitted to stop where there are yellow lines near the edge of the road?	
	8. Only to let passengers board or alight, or to load and unload goods (unless there are kerb marks to prohibit loading). I may park outside the hours shown on the plates.
9. Mark up the check list at the front of the book.	

STOPPING SAFELY

Questions	Answers
1. What two elements make up 'stopping distances'?	1. (a) Thinking distance. (b) Braking distance.
2. What is the 'thinking distance'?	2. It is the distance a car will go in the time it takes the brain to appreciate the danger, and apply the brakes.
3. What is the normal time on which 'thinking distance' is based?	3. 0.7 of a second, but where distractions occur this time could be longer and the 'thinking distance' would be greater.
4. Repeat the 'thinking distances' table.	4. 20 m.p.h. = 20 feet = 6 metres 30 m.p.h. = 30 feet = 9 metres 40 m.p.h. = 40 feet = 12 metres 50 m.p.h. = 50 feet = 15 metres 60 m.p.h. = 60 feet = 18 metres 70 m.p.h. = 70 feet = 21 metres
5. What is the 'braking distance'?	5. It is the distance a car will travel after braking, given good tyres, brakes and road conditions.
6. Repeat the 'braking distances' table.	6. 20 m.p.h. = 20 ft (same as the speed) = 6 m 30 m.p.h. = 45 ft (1$\frac{1}{2}$ times the speed) = 14 m 40 m.p.h. = 80 ft (2 times the speed) = 24 m 50 m.p.h. = 125 ft (2$\frac{1}{2}$ times speed) = 38 m 60 m.p.h. = 180 ft (3 times speed) = 55 m 70 m.p.h. = 245 ft (3$\frac{1}{2}$ times speed) = 75 m
7. What is the total stopping distance at 20 m.p.h.?	7. 40 feet = 12 metres
8. And at 30 m.p.h.?	8. 75 feet (2$\frac{1}{2}$ times the speed) = 23m
9. And at 40 m.p.h.?	9. 120 feet (3 times the speed) = 36 m
10. And at 50 m.p.h.?	10. 175 feet (3$\frac{1}{2}$ times the speed) = 53m
11. And at 60 m.p.h.?	11. 240 feet (4 times the speed) = 73 m
12. And at 70 m.p.h.?	12. 315 feet (4$\frac{1}{2}$ times the speed) = 96 m
13. What allowance should be made for wet roads, or icy roads?	13. (a) Leave at least twice the distance between me and the next car that I would leave in dry conditions. (b) Drive more slowly anyway.
14. Tick the check list	

MOTORWAYS

Questions	Answers
1. What are motorways?	1. They are dual carriageways with no intersections or cross-roads.
2. Who may **not** use motorways?	2. Pedestrians, cyclists, low powered motor cycles, slow moving and agricultural vehicles, invalid carriages under 5 cwt., animals, L-drivers and wide loads (unless authorised).
3. What is the chief feature of motorway traffic?	3. Faster speed.
4. When speeds are higher what does this require you to do?	4. (a) Ensure the vehicle is in good condition. (b) Assess road traffic situations more quickly. (c) Use the mirrors more frequently. (d) Keep a greater distance from the vehicle in front. (e) Concentrate all the time.
5. What particular points should you ensure about the condition of the vehicle?	5. (a) The radiator should be topped up and should not be masked off. (b) Sufficient petrol and oil should be available to get me to the next service station (about 25 miles). (c) The tyre pressures should be increased for sustained high speeds. (d) Loads carried or towed must be secure and evenly distributed.
6. How do you join a motorway?	6. There is a slip road on the left of the motorway, with an acceleration lane running alongside the inside lane.
7. Describe the actual manoeuvre of joining the motorway.	7. (a) Approach in the slip road. (b) Give way to traffic already on the motorway. (c) When a gap in the traffic in the left hand lane appears start off up the acceleration lane and speed up. (d) When travelling at the same speed as the traffic merge into the gap on the inside lane.
8. Which manoeuvres are forbidden on the motorway?	8. (a) Reversing (b) Turning in the road. (c) Crossing the central reserve. (d) Driving against the traffic.
9. Mark up the check list.	

MOTORWAY DRIVING

Questions	Answers
1. You have just joined the motorway. How long should you stay in the inside lane?	
2. What is the second lane of a two-lane carriageway for?	1. Until I have got used to the speed of the traffic.
3. What are the rules for a three-lane carriageway?	2. For overtaking only. I should drive in the left hand lane except when overtaking.
	3. (a) The left hand lane is for normal driving when the road ahead is clear. (b) I may stay in the middle lane if I am overtaking a succession of slower vehicles in the inside lane. (c) The outside lane is for overtaking only.
4. You have just passed a vehicle which was in the middle lane. What do you do?	
	4. (a) Return to the middle lane, but without cutting in, ahead of the vehicle I have overtaken. (b) If the road is clear of slow moving vehicles move over again into the left hand lane.
5. What are the rules about overtaking on the motorway?	
	5. (a) Overtake only on the right, unless traffic is queued up in slow moving lanes. (b) Never move to a lane to the left to overtake. (c) Never overtake on the hard shoulder. (d) Signal your intention to change lanes.
6. You find you have joined the motorway in the wrong direction, heading away from where you want to go. What do you do?	
	6. Carry on until the next exit from the motorway and decide on the best route from that point.
7. What is the commonest accident on motorways?	
	7. Rear-end collisions.
8. How can these be avoided?	
	8. (a) By keeping a safe distance from the vehicle in front. (b) By not overtaking unless it is clear a long way behind me. Fast traffic coming up behind is the main cause.
9. Mark up the check list at the front of the book.	

MOTORWAY SIGNALS

Questions	Answers
1. What does a flashing amber light mean on a motorway sign?	1. It means there are dangers ahead. I should reduce my speed and look out for danger.
2. What other indication may the flashing light give?	2. It may show a temporary maximum speed limit, lanes that are closed or a warning message – for example 'Fog'.
3. What do these signs mean?	3. They indicate emergency diversion routes for motorway traffic.
4. How can sleepiness on long drives be avoided?	4. (a) By ventilating the vehicle properly. (b) By stopping at a service area and having a short break. (c) By turning off at an exit and parking for a while. Walking around revives a sleepy driver.
(a) (b) (c) 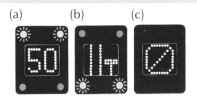5. Explain these motorway signals.	5. The amber flashing lights are warning lights of dangers ahead. (a) The 50 sign is the temporary maximum speed limit in the prevailing conditions. (b) This sign means that the overtaking lane ahead is closed for repairs, or perhaps because of an accident or broken-down vehicle. (c) This sign means the hazard is over; the road is now clear.
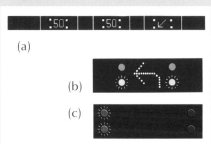6. Explain these motorways signals.	6. (a) Lane signals showing speed limits, and 'move over'. (b) Flashing amber lights show a hazard ahead. Leave the motorway at the next exit. (c) Flashing red lights mean 'proceed no further in this lane'.
7. Mark up the check list.	

FOG AND MOTORWAYS

Questions	Answers
1. What is the 'Fog Code'?	1. (a) Slow down. (b) Keep a safe distance. (c) Be able to pull up within my range of vision. (d) I must not hang on to someone else's tail lights. (e) I must not speed up to get away from someone who is too close behind me. (f) Watch my speed all the time. (g) If my vehicle is heavy I need longer to pull up. (h) Observe warning signals. (i) Use dipped lights or fog lamps. (j) Clean lights, windows, and reflectors whenever I can. (k) Allow more time for journeys in foggy weather. (l) Use my windscreen wipers and demister.
2. Why is fog such a serious hazard on motorways?	2. Fog is patchy; speeding up in clear places results in serious collisions in thick patches.
3. What particular difficulty with regard to leaving the motorway may occur in fog?	3. A motorist may not see the direction signs in time. I must keep a good look-out for my exit.
4. Slow moving vehicles in the left hand lane can assist here. How?	4. By letting other vehicles into the lane if they are trying to reach an exit.
5. What studs in the motorway help drivers at entrances and exits?	5. Green studs separate the acceleration and deceleration lanes from the through carriageway.
6. What other studs are used on the motorway?	6. (a) Red studs for the left hand edge of the carriageway. (b) Amber studs for the righthand edge of the central reservation.
7. Mark up the check list.	

HAZARDS ON MOTORWAYS

Questions	Answers
1. What is the speed limit on motorways?	1. Seventy miles per hour.
2. What precaution is necessary in wet, icy or foggy conditions?	2. Keep the speed down and a greater distance from the vehicle in front.
3. Your vehicle has broken down. What should you do if you are on a motorway?	3. (a) Get it off the carriageway onto the hard shoulder. (b) If I decide it is better for them to leave the car, keep my passengers well away from the carriageway. (c) Summon help by the roadside telephone system.
4. How can you tell where the nearest telephone is to be found?	4. Signs on the marker posts indicate the direction of the nearest telephone.
5. A lorry ahead of you has a red triangular sign. What are such signs?	5. They are projection markers showing overhanging loads.
6. What does a red triangle mean placed on the hard shoulder?	6. It means a broken down vehicle 150 metres further ahead.
7. You own a car telephone. What is the motorway rule?	7. I may not stop on the hard shoulder to answer or make a call, except in an emergency.
8. When may you stop on a motorway?	8. (a) When I break down. I then get onto the hard shoulder. (b) In an emergency – for example to prevent an accident. (c) Obeying a police signal. (d) When red lane lights are flashing and I cannot move to an alternative lane.
9. Where may you park on the motorway?	9. Only at the service areas.
10. What other areas on motorways are hazardous?	10. (a) Anywhere under repair. (b) Some link roads and slip roads have sharper bends than usual. I must lower my speed to negotiate them.
11. Mark up the check list at the front of the book.	

Questions	Answers
1. If you are walking on a motorway to a telephone box what must you be careful to do?	
	1. Never to walk on the carriageway.
2. Besides your passengers, who else might walk on the carriageway if you are not careful?	
	2. Household pets travelling with me. I must be very careful to secure pets so they cannot run on the carriageway.
3. How do you leave a motorway to turn left?	
	3. In the slip road provided.
4. How do you leave a motorway to turn right?	
	4. In the slip road on the left; then by bridge or a subway to turn right.
5. What are these signs?	
	5. They are the count-down markers, 300, 200 and 100 yards to the next exit.
6. How do you know when your exit is coming up?	
	6. Large signs indicate the junction slip roads and how far they are ahead. Then I watch for the count-down markers shown in question 5.
7. Go through the procedure for leaving the motorway.	
	7. (a) Eyes open for the sign telling me my junction is ahead. (b) Get into inside lane and give a left turn signal in good time. (c) Watch for the count-down markers. (d) Get into the deceleration lane and adjust my speed to non-motorway driving. (e) Leave by the slip road.
8. Too bad – you have missed your junction and gone 100 yards too far. What do you do?	
	8. It is essential to go on to the next junction. I must not stop, reverse, or turn back.
9. What is the great danger after leaving a motorway?	
	9. Failure to adjust to ordinary road conditions.
10. What in particular may need adjustment?	
	10. My speed will need watching – I must look at the speedometer frequently.
11. Mark up the check list.	

Questions	Answers

1. What does this sign mean?

1. It is the 'Start of the Motorway' sign.

2. What sign is this?

2. It is a route confirmatory sign. It appears after a junction to enable me to check that I am going in the correct direction.

3. Why are some direction signs placed over the motorway with downward pointing arrows?

3. They are the 'get in lane' signs for motorways.

4. What should you do when you see such 'get in lane' signs?

4. Move over in good time and then maintain lane discipline.

5. What is the white number 25 in the black box?

5. It is the number of the motorway junction I am approaching. It is useful in planning journeys, reporting breakdowns, etc.

6. When does a rectangular direction sign change to a pointer at one end?

6. At the junction, to point out the actual direction I should take.

7. Mark up the check list at the front of the book.

BREAKDOWNS

Questions	Answers
1. What do you do if you have a breakdown?	1. Get the vehicle off the road if possible.
2. Most cars have a special warning device. What is it?	2. The amber indicators can be made to flash on both sides at once as 'hazard warning lights' to warn other drivers.
3. What is the particular danger when broken down?	3. Other passing vehicles may hit drivers or passengers on the carriageway.
4. When pushing a vehicle at night what special danger is there?	4. I may obscure the rear lights of the car from other motorists.
5. What safety device can you carry to help when broken down?	5. A red triangle, which may be placed on the road 50 metres before the obstruction, on the same side of the road.
6. On motorways the red triangle should be placed a greater distance before the obstruction. How far on motorways?	6. One hundred and fifty metres.
7. Your vehicle carries traffic cones for emergency use. How should they be used?	7. To shield the broken down vehicle. The first one 15 metres from the obstruction next to the kerb; the last one level with the outside of the vehicle.
8. What should you do if anything falls from your vehicle?	8. Stop as soon as possible and retrieve it from the carriageway, with care, except on motorways where police assistance should be sought by telephone.
9. When you park, what is the correct position on the road?	9. As close as possible to the edge of the curb.
10. Before leaving the vehicle what should you do?	10. (a) Switch off the engine. (b) Apply the handbrake firmly. (c) Close the windows. (d) Switch off the headlamps if they have been in use. (e) Lock the vehicle, including the boot.
11. Mark up the check list.	

LEVEL CROSSINGS

Questions	Answers
1. What is a level crossing?	1. It is a place where the road crosses a railway line at the same level as the railway.
2. You should never drive 'nose to tail' over any level crossing. Why not?	2. If the vehicle in front of me stops I may be caught on the line.
3. When may you drive on to the crossing?	3. When I can see that my exit is clear.
4. The best rule for any level crossing is?	4. Drive over quickly. Never stop on, or immediately after, a crossing.
5. What are the four types of level crossing?	5. (a) Gated or full width barrier level crossings. (b) Automatic half barrier crossings. (c) Automatic open crossings. (d) Open crossings.

Questions	Answers
6. Describe these three signs that indicate level crossings.	6. (a) A red triangle with a gate on it indicates a gated or full width barrier crossing. (b) A red triangle with a steam engine indicates a level crossing, without gate or barrier, ahead. (c) A red St. Andrew's cross is used at all level crossings without barrier. The extra lower half of the cross indicates more than one line.
7. What is the essential rule for all level crossings of whatever type?	7. Always 'give way' to trains.
8. Some crossings have a yellow box junction marked on them. What does it mean?	8. Like all box junctions it means I must not enter the box until my exit is clear on the other side.
9. What special rules apply to horse riders when the warning starts?	9. (a) If I am on the crossing I go straight over. (b) If I am approaching I back well away from the crossing. I do not dismount.
10. Mark up the check list at the front of the book.	

AUTOMATIC HALF BARRIER CROSSINGS

Questions	Answers
1. What operates the automatic half barrier crossings?	
	1. The train itself – setting off warning lights and closing the barriers shortly before it reaches the crossing.
2. What warning is given?	
	2. Steady amber warning lights and bells warn of the danger at first. Then red stop lights flash when the barrier is about to come down.
3. What must you do when the amber lights come on and the bells ring?	
	3. Stop at once unless it is unsafe to do so.
4. And when the red lights flash?	
	4. Stop before, but as close to the white stop line as I can. I must never zig-zag round a barrier.
5. How much later will the train arrive?	
	5. The Code says "soon after the lights begin to show".
6. The train has gone past, yet the lights continue to flash. Is anything wrong?	
	6. No – but another train is coming.
7. What are the telephones for at this type of barrier?	
	7. (a) To phone the signalman if the barriers fail – they should never be down for more than three minutes. (b) To phone the signalman if I break down on the crossing or if I am driving a wide, long or slow-moving vehicle, or herding animals.
8. You break down on the crossing. What do you do?	
	8. (i) Get the passengers out of the vehicle and clear of the crossing. (ii) Phone the signalman at once. (iii) If possible, push the vehicle clear of the crossing, or drive off on the starter after telephoning. (iv) If the bells start, or the red lights flash, I stand well clear of the crossing.
9. If you are on the crossing and the amber lights come on, and the bells ring, what do you do?	
	9. Keep going.
10. What do these signs indicate?	
	10. The markers show how far it is to a concealed level crossing.
11. Mark up the check list.	

MORE ABOUT LEVEL CROSSINGS

Questions	Answers
1. What is an automatic open crossing?	1. It is a crossing without gates, barriers or attendants, but it does have amber lights, an audible alarm and flashing red 'STOP' lights.
2. What are the rules for this type of crossing?	2. (a) Never cross the line if the lights are showing and the alarm sounds. (b) Continued flashing and alarm bells means that another train is coming. (c) Use the telephone (if available) if I have a long vehicle or am herding animals, and use it on the other side after crossing, to confirm I am safely over the lines.
3. Are there any difficulties with attended crossings?	3. Not usually, since the attendant opens and closes the gates.
4. What about unattended crossings with lights? What are the rules?	4. (a) Never cross when the lights are red, a train is coming. (b) If the lights are green open both gates; drive over; stop on the other side and close both gates. Never drive onto the lines before opening the exit gate.
5. What about the special telephone provided?	5. This is used to phone the signal box for permission to cross, by persons: (a) driving wide vehicles. (b) driving long vehicles. (c) driving slow moving vehicles. (d) herding animals. Phone him again when all is clear.
6. What about open level crossings, which have no gates, no attendants and no lights; all they have is a 'give way' sign.	6. (a) Stop. (b) Look both ways and listen for a train. (c) Always 'give way' to trains.
7. Mark up the check list at the beginning of the book.	

TRAFFIC LIGHTS

Questions	Answers
1. What is the correct sequence for traffic lights? Start with red.	1. (a) Red. (b) Red and amber together. (c) Green. (d) Amber. (e) Red.
2. Now give the sequence again, but starting with green.	2. (a) Green. (b) Amber. (c) Red. (d) Red and Amber together. (e) Green.
3. What does the red light mean?	3. Stop. I must not cross the stop line on the carriageway.
4. What do 'red and amber together' mean?	4. This also means 'stop'. I must not cross the stop line until the green light appears.
5. What does the green light mean?	5. It means I may go if the way is clear.
6. The green light is showing but you are turning left. What is the rule?	6. I must give way to pedestrians crossing the road I wish to enter.
7. What does the amber light on its own mean?	7. It means 'stop'. I must stop at the stop line. I may only proceed if: (a) I have already crossed the stop line, or (b) if it would be dangerous for me to stop.
8. You are in a left filter lane. The light is red but the filter arrow is at green. May you filter to the left?	8. Yes – I may filter left when the green arrow is on no matter what the other lights say, provided my way is clear.
9. Mark up the check list at the front of the book.	

Questions	Answers
1. What Act of Parliament controls the licensing of vehicles?	1. The Vehicle (Excise) Act.
2. Is it an offence to use an unlicensed vehicle?	2. Yes.
3. Where can you renew a licence?	3. At any vehicle licensing centre, or at branch Post Offices.
4. What other documents do you need besides a Road Fund Licence before you can take a vehicle on the road?	4. (a) A driving licence. (b) A valid test certificate if the vehicle is old enough to need one. (c) A Certificate of Motor Insurance.
5. What is a valid driving licence?	5. It is a driving licence which: (a) covers the class of vehicle I am driving. (b) is for a current period, i.e. it is not out of date. (c) I have signed it at the bottom with my ordinary signature.
6. You are asked by the police to produce your driving licence but have left it at home by mistake. What is your position?	6. I may produce it within five days at any police station I select.
7. What is a valid test certificate?	7. An M.O.T. (Ministry of Transport) certificate is required when vehicles are more than three years old. It is issued by certified garages which are authorised to conduct the test. It lasts one year.
8. Your car fails to pass the test because of faulty steering. What should be done?	8. The garage will repair it and issue the certificate when the vehicle is again roadworthy, if I agree to pay for the repair.
9. What is a valid insurance policy?	9. One that covers at least third party claims, that is claims by pedestrians, passengers, motorists and other people suffering loss by my negligence.
10. What is a comprehensive policy?	10. 'Comprehensive' means 'including much'. It covers a wider range of risks than a third party policy, but not necessarily every risk.
11. Mark up the check list.	

Questions	Answers
1. What is the rule about eyesight?	1. I must meet the official eyesight standard, wearing glasses or contact lenses if necessary.
2. What are the requirements about vehicle condition?	2. The vehicle, and any trailer, must be in such a condition as not to cause any danger either to me or to others.
3. What preparations are necessary for winter driving?	3. Check the battery, and use anti-freeze in the radiator and windscreen washer bottle.
4. What is the requirement for brakes and steering?	4. They must be in good working order and properly adjusted.
5. What are the rules about tyres, including the spare?	5. (a) They must be suitable for the vehicle. (b) Properly inflated. (c) Have a tread of at least 1.6mm. (d) And be free from cuts and defects. (e) Radial and crossply types must never be mixed on the same axle. If radial tyres are used on only one axle they must be at the back.
6. What are the requirements about windscreens and windscreen wipers?	6. (a) The windscreen must be clean. (b) The windscreen wipers must be in working order.
7. What is the requirement about your horn?	7. It must be in working order so that I can warn other drivers of my presence.
8. Your speedometer is not working. Is it an offence?	8. Yes, it is an offence against the Construction and Use Regulations.
9. What is a silencer, and what are the rules about it?	9. A silencer is a device which has baffle plates fitted into it to reduce the sound of the engine explosions. It must be efficient.
10. What are the rules about the load on a vehicle?	10. (a) It must not be excessive. (b) It must be distributed properly. (c) It must be secure.
11. What about wide loads?	11. The load must not be of illegal width as laid down in the Construction and Use Regulations.
12. Mark up the check list.	

SEAT BELTS AND OTHER MATTERS

Questions	Answers
1. Who must wear a seat belt?	1. Drivers and all passengers where seat belts are fitted, unless exempt.
2. Whose responsibility is it to see that seat belts are worn?	2. Chiefly the driver's and he must ensure his passengers know how to use the seat belts. Adults travelling on rear seats are themselves liable if they fail to use the seat belts provided.
3. Who is exempt?	3. Holders of a medical exemption certificate; drivers who are reversing and local deliverymen in a vehicle constructed for that purpose.
4. How should children be restrained in a car?	4. Preferably on the back seat, wearing approved child restraint devices.
5. What are approved child restraint devices?	5. (a) Under 1 year old – an infant carrier or a carrycot held by straps. (b) 1, 2 or 3 year olds – a child safety seat or harness, or a booster cushion with an adult seat. (c) 4-14 years – an appropriate child seat or harness or an adult belt, with or without a booster cushion.
6. Where should children not be carried?	6. In the luggage space of an estate car, or hatchback, unless seats are provided.
7. What are the rules for winter driving?	7. (a) In icy conditions drive with care even if the roads have been gritted. (b) Take care when overtaking gritting vehicles. (c) Do not drive in snow unless the journey is essential. (d) Keep in as high a gear as possible to reduce wheel spin. (e) Use headlights in snow.
8. Mark up the check list provided at the front of the book.	

SKIDDING

Questions	Answers
1. What are the chief causes of skidding?	1. (a) Incorrect braking. (b) Incorrect steering. (c) Incorrect acceleration.
2. You get into a skid because of bad road conditions. Are you to blame?	2. Yes – because I am required to drive according to road and traffic conditions.
3. Why does a braking skid occur?	3. The driver is asking more of the car in braking performance than it can manage in the road conditions.
4. What is the effect of heavy braking?	4. (a) The weight of the car is thrown forward onto the front wheels. (b) The rear wheels, having less weight on them, lose their grip. (c) These wheels lock and the car starts to swing.
5. What is the additional danger to heavy braking in an emergency?	5. Steering to avoid other vehicles can induce a skid.
6. Why does steering affect skidding?	6. It throws further weight onto the front wheel on the outside of the turn, and decreases the weight still more on the back wheels.
7. What is the danger when a car spins?	7. It may turn over if it hits anything.
8. How can you prevent skids?	8. (a) Keep speeds down especially when road conditions are bad. (b) Take proper note of triangular warning signs about bends, slippery roads, etc. (c) Maintain the vehicle properly.
9. What corrective action can you take?	9. Cease braking, and steer into the skid, that is if the rear of the car swings to the right I steer to the right.
10. What does this do?	10. It brings the front wheels back in line with the rear wheels.
11. Mark up the check list.	

ROUTE SIGNS

Questions	Answers
1. What are direction signs like?	

1. What are direction signs like?

2. Explain this direction sign.

3. And this?

4. And this?

5. What happens to the direction sign at a junction?

6. What is this sign?

(A 46)

7. What does a route in brackets mean?

8. Explain this sign.

9. How many did you get right? Put a tick on the check list at the front of this book.

Answers

1. They are mostly rectangular. If they refer to primary routes they have a green background. If they refer to other routes they have white backgrounds. Blue borders refer to local routes.

2. (a) It refers to a primary route.
(b) The road dead ahead is a 'No Entry' road.
(c) The primary route A6 forks to the left.

3. (a) It refers to non-primary routes.
(b) Slough lies to the right.
(c) Datchet and Windsor, the B470, are slightly left at eleven o'clock.
(d) The London Road, the A4, is a turning off the Datchet/Windsor road.

4. (a) Blue borders – local routes.
(b) The towns named lie in the directions indicated at the distances shown in miles.

5. One end of it is pointed to point down the correct turning.

6. A direction sign to a tourist attraction.

7. It means that this route can be reached at a turning off from the main route indicated.

8. It indicates a primary route ring-road, i.e. one skirting the centre of a town for through traffic wishing to avoid congestion.

Questions	Answers

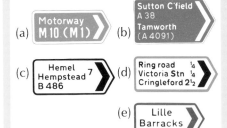

(a) Motorway M10 (M1)
(b) Sutton C'field A 38 Tamworth (A 4091)
(c) Hemel Hempstead 7 B 486
(d) Ring road ¼ Victoria Stn ¼ Cringleford 2½
(e) Lille Barracks

1.   Explain these signs.

A 46
Lincoln   12
Newark   28
(Nottingham 48)
Leicester   63

2.   Explain this sign.

Public Library
Council Offices

3.   And this.

4.   What are these overhead signs?

5.   What colour signs mark routes for diverted traffic?

6.   How many did you score out of five? Tick the check list.

---

1.   (a) Directional sign to motorway.
     (b) Primary route directional sign.
     (c) Non-primary route directional sign.
     (d) Directional route to local places.
     (e) Ministry of Defence establishments have directional signs with red borders.

2.   This is a primary route confirmatory sign. It reassures drivers that they are on the right route. (A confirmatory sign on a secondary route is black on a white background.)

3.   This is a sign to show pedestrians the best route to follow. It does not apply to drivers.

4.   They are lane control signs. Red crosses show lanes closed to traffic facing the sign.

5.   Black writing on a yellow background.

ACCIDENTS

Questions	Answers
1. You are involved in an accident. Do you need to stop?	
2. What does the Road Traffic Act mean by animal?	1. Yes – if it causes injury or damage to any other person, vehicle or animal.
	2. A horse, ass, mule, sheep, cattle, pig, goat, or dog not in my own vehicle.
3. What must you do besides stop?	
	3. (a) Remain long enough to enable any person having reasonable grounds for requiring them to obtain my name and address, the vehicle owner's name and address and the registration mark of the vehicle.
4. If you do not give your name and address to any such person at the time, what must you do?	(b) If anyone is injured, the accident must be reported to the police.
5. What else should you produce if anyone is injured?	4. Report the accident to the police within 24 hours.
6. You are first on the scene of an accident. What do you do?	5. My insurance certificate, either when reporting the accident or within 5 days thereafter.
	6. (a) Warn other traffic with flashing signs or by putting out a red triangle. (b) Summon police and ambulance authorities, giving precise details of location and casualties. (c) Prevent fire by enforcing a no-smoking rule and asking drivers to switch off engines. (d) Render first aid as required, moving casualties only if in further danger. (e) Get other passengers out of the vehicle to a place of safety. (f) Remain at the scene until emergency services arrive.
7. The vehicle involved is marked with one of the 'hazardous load' plates. What do you do?	
	7. Note the contents of the vehicle and the type of sign and include these details when I summon the emergency services. I use care in any 'rescue' operations if liquids, gases or powders may cause danger.
8. Mark up the check list at the beginning of the book.	

MORE ABOUT ACCIDENTS

Questions	Answers
1. What is the best sequence of activities to help in an accident?	1. (a) Deal with danger. (b) Summon help. (c) Give First Aid.
2. What are the chief dangers in a road accident?	2. (a) Further collisions. (b) Fire.
3. The quickest aid to warn other drivers is...?	3. My own hazard warning lights, if my car is fitted with them.
4. The other helpful warning device is...?	4. The red triangle warning sign. I should carry one with me all the time.
5. How can fire be prevented?	5. (a) Switch off all engines. (b) Impose a strict 'No Smoking' ban.
6. How can you summon help?	6. (a) Send a bystander if there is one. (b) On a motorway ask a driver coming up to drive round the obstacle and go on to the next telephone.
7. What information should be given to the emergency services?	7. (a) The location of the accident. (b) The number of vehicles involved. (c) Whether an ambulance is required. (d) How many casualties are involved. (e) If a 'diamonds for danger' vehicle is involved what the diamond plate says about the nature of the goods being carried.
8. Go over this page very carefully. Then mark up the check list.	

FIRST AID IN ACCIDENTS

Questions	Answers
1. A victim is unconscious but breathing. What do you do until help arrives?	
	1. (a) I do not move the victim unless he/she is in danger. (b) I watch to make sure breathing continues. (c) I cover the victim to keep him/her warm.
2. A victim is unconscious and breathing has stopped. What do you do?	
	2. (a) I remove any obvious obstruction in the mouth. (b) I keep the victim's head tilted backwards as far as possible. (c) If breathing does not start and the victim's colour does not improve I pinch the nostrils and breathe into the victim's mouth until the chest rises. Then I withdraw and repeat the action every four seconds until natural breathing starts.
3. A victim is bleeding. What do you do?	
	3. (a) Apply firm pressure over the wound, preferably with some clean material. (b) Secure a pad if possible with a bandage or length of cloth. (c) I avoid pressure on any foreign body in the wound. (d) If limbs are unbroken raising the limb may lessen the bleeding.
4. Some casualties are in vehicles, but in no danger. What do you do about them?	
	4. Leave them in the vehicle until the emergency services arrive.
5. What is the cardinal rule about victims drinking?	
	5. Never give an accident victim anything to drink.
6. Casualties are shocked. What do you do?	
	6. (a) Re-assure them that expert help is coming. (b) Keep them comfortable as possible. (c) Keep them warm. (d) See they are not left alone.
7. What positive contributions can everyone make in times of accidents?	
	7. (a) Carry a First Aid kit always. (b) Learn First Aid. (c) Know what to do and do it efficiently.
8. (a) Mark up the check list. (b) Go out and buy a First Aid kit and a red triangle if you haven't one.	

Questions	Answers
1. You are at a junction controlled by a traffic warden. He is holding up the traffic going straight ahead. You wish to filter left. May you do so?	1. No – not unless the warden signals that I may do so.
2. The traffic lights are green, but your exit from the junction controlled by the lights is not clear. What do you do?	2. I must not go forward until I can clear the junction.
3. The red and amber lights are showing together. May you go forward?	3. No.
4. The traffic lights have a green filter signal. What is the rule?	4. Do not get into the green filter lane unless I wish to go in the direction shown by the filter arrow.
(a) (b) 5. What do these warning signs mean?	5. (a) Road works ahead. (b) Change to opposite carriageway ahead. (May be reversed).
(a) REDUCE SPEED NOW (b) (c) 6. Explain these three signs.	6. (a) The 'reduce speed now' sign is shown on some signs where hazards are being approached. (b) Route deviates sharply to the left. (c) Route deviates sharply to the right.
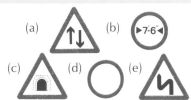 7. What do these signs mean?	7. (a) Two-way traffic ahead. (b) Width of vehicle limited to 7'6". (c) Tunnel. (d) All vehicles prohibited – play street. A plate will state the hours, and also whether vehicles may enter for access to properties. (e) Double bend; first to the left. (May be reversed).
8. Go over these again until you are sure of them all. Tick the check list.	

ALCOHOL AND OTHER MATTERS

Questions	Answers
1. What effect does alcohol have on driving ability?	1. It increases reaction time, impairs judgment of speed, distance and risk, and inspires a false sense of confidence.
2. What is the safest course as far as alcohol is concerned?	2. If I am going to drive I should not drink.
3. What is the legal limit of alcohol?	3. 35 microgrammes of alcohol per 100 millilitres of breath.
4. What proportion of road deaths are alcohol related?	4. About one third of all road deaths are of persons who are over the legal limit.
5. What is the penalty for driving above the legal limit?	5. Disqualification for a long period and possibly a heavy fine and imprisonment.
6. What restrictions are placed on invalid carriages?	6. Invalid carriages under 5 cwt. may not be used on motorways.
7. Why should you give invalid carriages special consideration?	7. Because a handicapped person may find it difficult to adjust as quickly as myself to road and traffic conditions.
8. A vehicle is approaching you in broad daylight with its headlights full on. What may this mean?	8. A special hazard is approaching. Very often it is a 'wide load' or a 'long load' travelling by special authorisation under police escort.
9. What does the Code say about tinted glasses and windows?	9. Never use any type of tinted glasses at night, or in bad visibility. Do not use tinting materials on windows.
10. You break down at night, and have to walk to a garage. What should you remember?	10. To wear, or carry, something white.
11. Mark up the check list.	

Questions	Answers
1. Ahead of you, you see a flashing amber sign. What could it be?	1. (a) A pelican crossing. (b) A driver signalling a manoeuvre. (c) If it is school opening or closing time it could warn of a school crossing patrol ahead. (d) It could be a broken-down vehicle. (e) It could be a towing vehicle, a gritting vehicle or some similar vehicle. (f) On a motorway it could be the old type of flashing amber sign; reduce speed to 30 m.p.h. until the danger is passed. (g) On motorways it could be the new overhead lane signals imposing speed limits or warning of hazards ahead.
2. Ahead of you, you see flashing red signs. What could they mean?	2. (a) The 'stop' warnings at a level crossing, lifting bridge, airfield, fire station or other place where traffic has to be interrupted as and when necessary. (b) The motorway 'lane closed' sign.
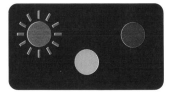	
3. What do these signs mean?	3. I must stop at the signal.
4. Ahead of you, you see flashing purple-blue lights. What are they?	4. These are the emergency lights used on police vehicles, ambulances, etc. I must be ready to stop, or give way as necessary, and should be prepared to co-operate if requested to assist.
5. Mark up the check list.	

BUS LANES, TRAMS AND CYCLE LANES

Questions	Answers
1. What is a bus lane?	1. It is a lane on one side of a road reserved at certain times for the use of buses, cyclists and possibly other vehicles such as taxis.
2. What is the idea of bus lanes?	2. To speed up buses and thus encourage travel by bus, which reduces road congestion.
3. In one-way streets bus lanes can present a special problem. What is it?	3. The bus lane may be a contraflow lane so that I might find a bus travelling towards me against the one-way flow (but in its own lane which I must not enter).
4. What are the rules about tramways?	4. (a) I must not enter a road or lane reserved for trams. (b) Always give way to trams. (c) Take extra care where the tramlines cross from one side of the road to the other.
5. What is the particular danger at tram stops?	5. (a) If the tram stop has a platform, I must follow the directions given by road markings and signs. (b) If there is no platform, I must not drive between the tram and the left-hand kerb where passengers are waiting to board.
6. What special parking rule applies to roads where trams run?	6. I must not park where my vehicle would get in the way of trams, or cause other vehicles to do so.
7. What is a cycle lane?	7. A special lane reserved for cyclists. I may not drive on the lane if the white line is unbroken. If it is a broken line I should not enter the lane if I can avoid doing so.
 8. What do these road markings indicate?	8. The presence of a road hump deliberately installed to force vehicles to reduce speed.
9. Mark up the check list.	

THE FINAL PAGE — SUNDRY ITEMS

Questions	Answers
1. It is an offence to park a vehicle on Common Land ....(continue the rule)	1. .....more than ten metres from a highway.
2. What shape are signs that give information?	2. Rectangular.
3. What colour are they?	3. They have blue backgrounds.

Questions	Answers
4. What does this sign mean?	4. Tourist information available in direction shown.

5. What does this sign mean?

5. Parking restricted to use by people named on the sign.

6. And this sign?

6. Hospital ahead.

7. And this sign?

7. Parking permitted on verge or footway.

8. Explain this sign.

8. No through road.

9. What is a 'no through road'?

9. A road which is closed off at the far end and is only available therefore for access and parking.

10. Explain this sign.

10. Traffic in my lane has priority over traffic from the opposite direction. It is used in narrow roads.

11. Explain this sign.

11. I must give way to vehicles travelling towards me.

12. The end! Good luck with your test! When you have passed it remember that as traffic increases the Code becomes more and more important. Care, consideration and courtesy are the foundations of safe driving. It is your attitude, not just your aptitude, that counts.

INDEX